I0821667

NORTH AMERICA

by Claire Vanden Branden

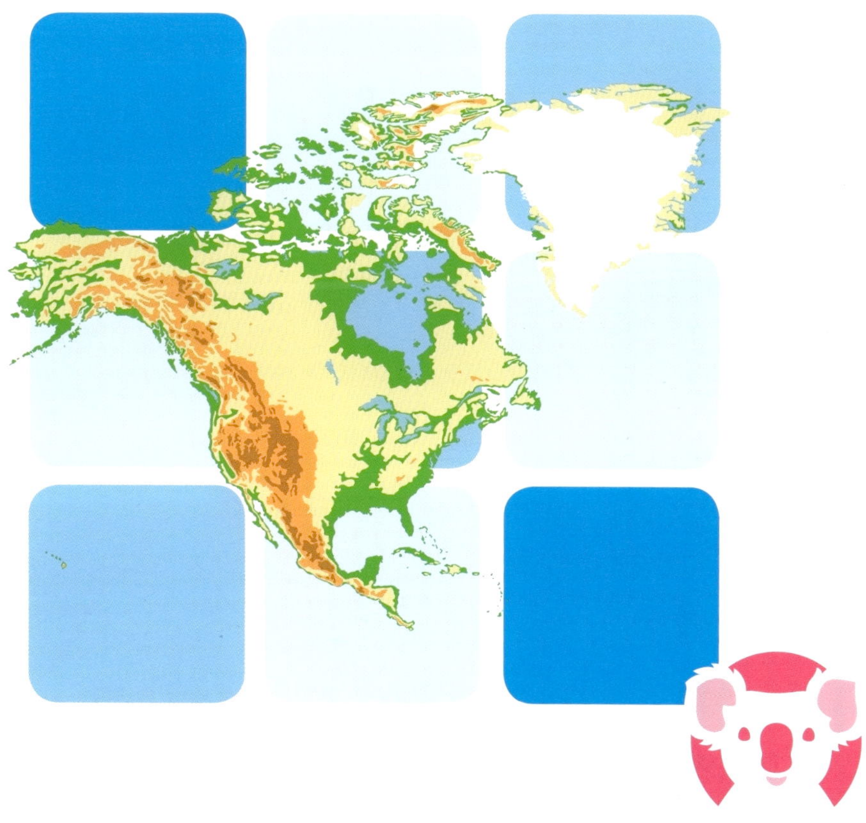

Cody Koala
An Imprint of Pop!
popbooksonline.com

abdobooks.com
Published by Pop!, a division of ABDO, PO Box 398166, Minneapolis, Minnesota 55439.

Printed in the United States of America, North Mankato, Minnesota.

092018
012019

THIS BOOK CONTAINS RECYCLED MATERIALS

Cover Photo: Shutterstock Images
Interior Photos: Shutterstock Images, 1, 5 (top), 5 (bottom right), 9, 10, 13 (bottom left), 13 (bottom right), 14, 21; iStockphoto, 5 (bottom left); Red Line Editorial, 6; Design Pics Inc/Alamy, 13 (top); David McNew/AFP/Getty Images, 17; Alan Rogers/The Casper Star-Tribune/AP Images, 18

Editor: Charly Haley
Series Designer: Laura Mitchell

Library of Congress Control Number: 2018949780

Publisher's Cataloging-in-Publication Data
Names: Vanden Branden, Claire, author.
Title: North America / by Claire Vanden Branden.
Description: Minneapolis, Minnesota: Pop!, 2019 | Series: Continents | Includes online resources and index.
Identifiers: ISBN 9781532161742 (lib. bdg.) | ISBN 9781641855457 (pbk) | ISBN 9781532162800 (ebook)
Subjects: LCSH: North America--Juvenile literature. | Continents--Juvenile literature. | Geography--Juvenile literature.
Classification: DDC 917--dc23

Hello! My name is

Cody Koala

Pop open this book and you'll find QR codes like this one, loaded with information, so you can learn even more!

Scan this code* and others like it while you read, or visit the website below to make this book pop.

popbooksonline.com/north-america

*Scanning QR codes requires a web-enabled smart device with a QR code reader app and a camera.

Table of Contents

Chapter 1

North America

North America is the third-largest **continent** in the world. It has 23 countries. It touches the Pacific Ocean, Atlantic Ocean, and Arctic Ocean.

Watch a video here!

MAP OF
NORTH AMERICA
GREENLAND
ARCTIC
OCEAN
CANADA
PACIFIC
OCEAN
MISSISSIPPI RIVER
ROCKY MOUNTAINS
UNITED STATES
APPALACHIAN MOUNTAINS
ATLANTIC
OCEAN
MEXICO
CENTRAL
AMERICA
1. GUATEMALA
2. BELIZE
3. EL SALVADOR
4. HONDURAS
5. NICARAGUA
6. COSTA RICA
7. PANAMA
8. CUBA
9. CAYMAN ISLANDS
10. JAMAICA
11. THE BAHAMAS
12. HAITI
13. DOMINICAN REPUBLIC
14. PUERTO RICO
15. VIRGIN ISLANDS
16. ANGUILLA
17. ST. MARTIN
18. BARBUDA
19. ANTIGUA
20. MONTSERRAT
21. GUADELOUPE
22. DOMINICA
23. ST. LUCIA
24. BARBADOS
25. ST. VINCENT
26. GRENADA
27. TRINIDAD AND TOBAGO

Part of North America is called Central America. It connects North America to another continent called South America.

Greenland is in North America. It is the biggest island in the world.

Chapter 2

Different Landscapes

North America has many different **landscapes**. Mexico has deserts. Central America is **tropical**.

Learn more here!

Great Plains in South Dakota

The United States and Canada have flat grassland called the Great Plains. The Rocky Mountains are in the west. The Appalachian Mountains are in the east.

The Mississippi River is the largest river system in North America. Many rivers flow into the Mississippi.

Chapter 3

Animals and Plants

Many different animals live in North America. Mountains are home to wolverines. Armadillos live in warm areas. Moose live in forests.

Learn more here!

Many kinds of plants live in North America. Cacti grow in the hot deserts. Orchid flowers grow in the tropical forests.

A bristlecone pine tree in California is more than 5,000 years old. It's the oldest tree in the world.

Chapter 4

People of North America

Indigenous Peoples have lived in North America for thousands of years. They lived there before anyone else.

Oodham
Complete an activity here!

In the 1400s, people from Europe started moving to North America. They took land away from the Indigenous Peoples over many years.

Today, many Indigenous people work to continue their **traditions** from before Europeans came.

People with **heritages** from all around the world live in North America today. Many big cities have neighborhoods featuring different heritages. Some cities have Chinatown, Koreatown, or Little Italy.

Chinatown in San Francisco, California

Making Connections

Text-to-Self

There are different landscapes in North America. What is the landscape like where you live? Is it flat? Are there mountains?

Text-to-Text

Have you read another book about North America? What did you learn?

Text-to-World

The people who were native to North America had their land taken by Europeans. Why do you think it's important to tell their stories?

Glossary

continent – one of the seven large landmasses on Earth.

heritage – personal history passed down through families and groups of people.

Indigenous People – the first group of people in an area.

landscape – the natural features of an area of land.

tradition – a belief or way of doing things that is passed down to different people over time.

tropical – very hot.

Index

Online Resources

popbooksonline.com

Thanks for reading this Cody Koala book!

Scan this code* and others like it in this book, or visit the website below to make this book pop!

*Scanning QR codes requires a web-enabled smart device with a QR code reader app and a camera.